C A N A D I A N B R A S S
SERIES OF
COLLECTED QUINTETS

EASY CLASSICS

arranged for brass quintet
by Charles Sayre

T005590u

contents

Welcome to the new *Canadian Brass Series of Collected Quintets*. In our work with students we have for some time been aware of the need for more brass quintet music at easy and intermediate levels of difficulty. We are continually observing a kind of "Renaissance" in brass music, not only in audience responses to our quintet, but to all brass music in general. The brass quintet, as a chamber ensemble, seems to have become as standard a chamber combination as a string quartet. That could not have been said twenty-five years ago. Brass quintets are popping up everywhere — professional quintets, junior and senior high school ensembles, college and university groups, and amateur quintets of adult players.

We have carefully chosen the literature for these collected quintets, and closely supervised the arrangements. Our aim was to retain a Canadian Brass flavor to each arrangement, and create attractive repertory designed so that any brass quintet can play it with satisfying results. We've often remarked to one another that we certainly wish that we'd had quintet arrangements like these when we were students!

Happy playing to you and your quintet.

THE CANADIAN BRASS

HAL•LEONARD®
CORPORATION
7777 W. BLUEMOUND RD. P.O. BOX 13819 MILWAUKEE, WI 53213

C A N A D I A N
B R A S S
SERIES OF
COLLECTED QUINTETS

Exciting repertory books of quintets, containing a wide variety of literature. These easy and intermediate collections retain the flavor of Canadian Brass recorded repertory, and the selection of the music and the arrangements for this series were supervised by the Canadian Brass.

Easy level (1-3 years experience);

Easy Classics
arranged by Charles Sayre
Contents: Two Chorales — O Sacred Head, and Break Forth, O Beauteous Heavenly Light (Bach); Two Fuguing Tunes — When Jesus Wept and Kittery (Billings); Victorious Love (Gastoldi); In the Hall of the Mountain King (Grieg); Austrian Hymn (Haydn); Canon (Tallis).

50488760 Trumpet I
50488761 Trumpet II
50488762 Horn in F
50488763 Trombone
50488764 Tuba
50488765 Conductor's Score

Hymns for Brass
Contents: Ah, Holy Jesus; Beautiful Saviour; Christ the Lord Is Risen Today; Eternal Father, Strong to Save; A Mighty Fortress Is Our God; We Gather Together.

50488754 Trumpet I
50488755 Trumpet II
50488756 Horn in F
50488757 Trombone
50488758 Tuba
50488759 Conductor's Score

Rodgers and Hammerstein Hits
arranged by Charles Sayre
Contents: Edelweiss *(The Sound of Music);* Oklahoma *(Oklahoma);* You'll Never Walk Alone *(Carousel);* Oh, What a Beautiful Morning *(Oklahoma);* Blow High, Blow Low *(Carousel);* Honey Bun *(South Pacific).*

50488766 Trumpet I
50488767 Trumpet II
50488768 Horn in F
50488769 Trombone
50488770 Tuba
50488771 Conductor's Score

Intermediate level (4 years or more playing experience):

Brass on Broadway
arranged by Bob Lowden
Contents: Broadway Baby *(Follies)*; Comedy Tonight *(A Funny Thing Happened on the Way to the Forum)*; Get Me to the Church on Time *(My Fair Lady)*; Ol' Man River *(Show Boat)*: Sunrise, Sunset *(Fiddler on the Roof);* They Call the Wind Maria *(Paint Your Wagon).*

50488778 Trumpet I
50488779 Trumpet II
50488780 Horn in F
50488781 Trombone
50488782 Tuba
50488783 Conductor's Score

Favorite Classics
arranged by Henry Charles Smith
Contents: Gavotte from the Sixth Cello Suite (Bach); Prayer from *Hansel and Gretel* (Humperdinck); Cantate Domino (Pitoni); TheLiberty Bell (Sousa); Questo e quella from Rigoletto (Verdi); Pilgrim's Chorus from *Tannhauser* (Wagner).

50488784 Trumpet I
50488785 Trumpet II
50488786 Horn in F
50488787 Trombone
50488788 Tuba
50488789 Conductor's Score

Immortal Folksongs
arranged by Terry Vosbein
Contents: Greensleeves; High Barbary; Londonderry Air; Shenandoah; Simple Gifts; The Drunken Sailor.

50488772 Trumpet I
50488773 Trumpet II
50488774 Horn in F
50488775 Trombone
50488776 Tuba
50488777 Conductor's Score

TWO CHORALES

1. O Sacred Head

J. S. Bach
(1685-1750)
arranged by Charles Sayre

Legato tongue throughout unless otherwise slurred.

2. Break Forth, O Beauteous Heavenly Light

TWO FUGUING TUNES
1. When Jesus Wept

William Billings
(1746-1800)
arranged by Charles Sayre

2. Kittery

VICTORIOUS LOVE
(Amor Vittorioso)

Giovanni Giacomo Gastoldi
(c1550- c1622)
arranged by Charles Sayre

Play through the piece twice.

IN THE HALL OF THE MOUNTAIN KING

Edvard Grieg
(1843-1907)
arranged by Charles Sayre

Sempre Staccato

AUSTRIAN HYMN

Franz Joseph Haydn
(1732-1809)
arranged by Charles Sayre

* Legato Tongue Throughout except where slurred or otherwise indicated

CANON

Thomas Tallis
(c1505-1585)
arranged by Charles Sayre

*Legato Tongue all note,
unless otherwise indicated*

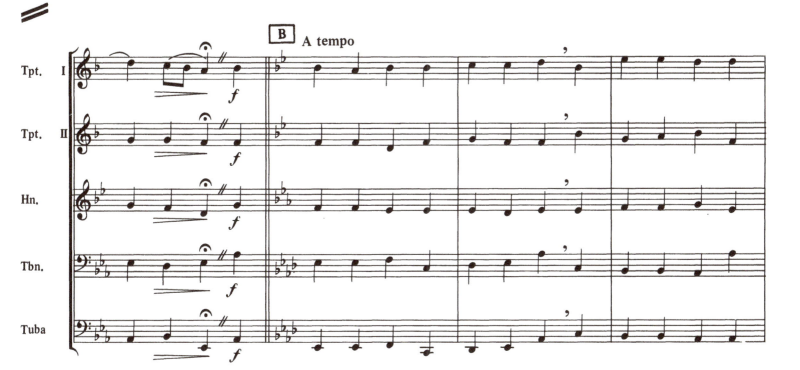